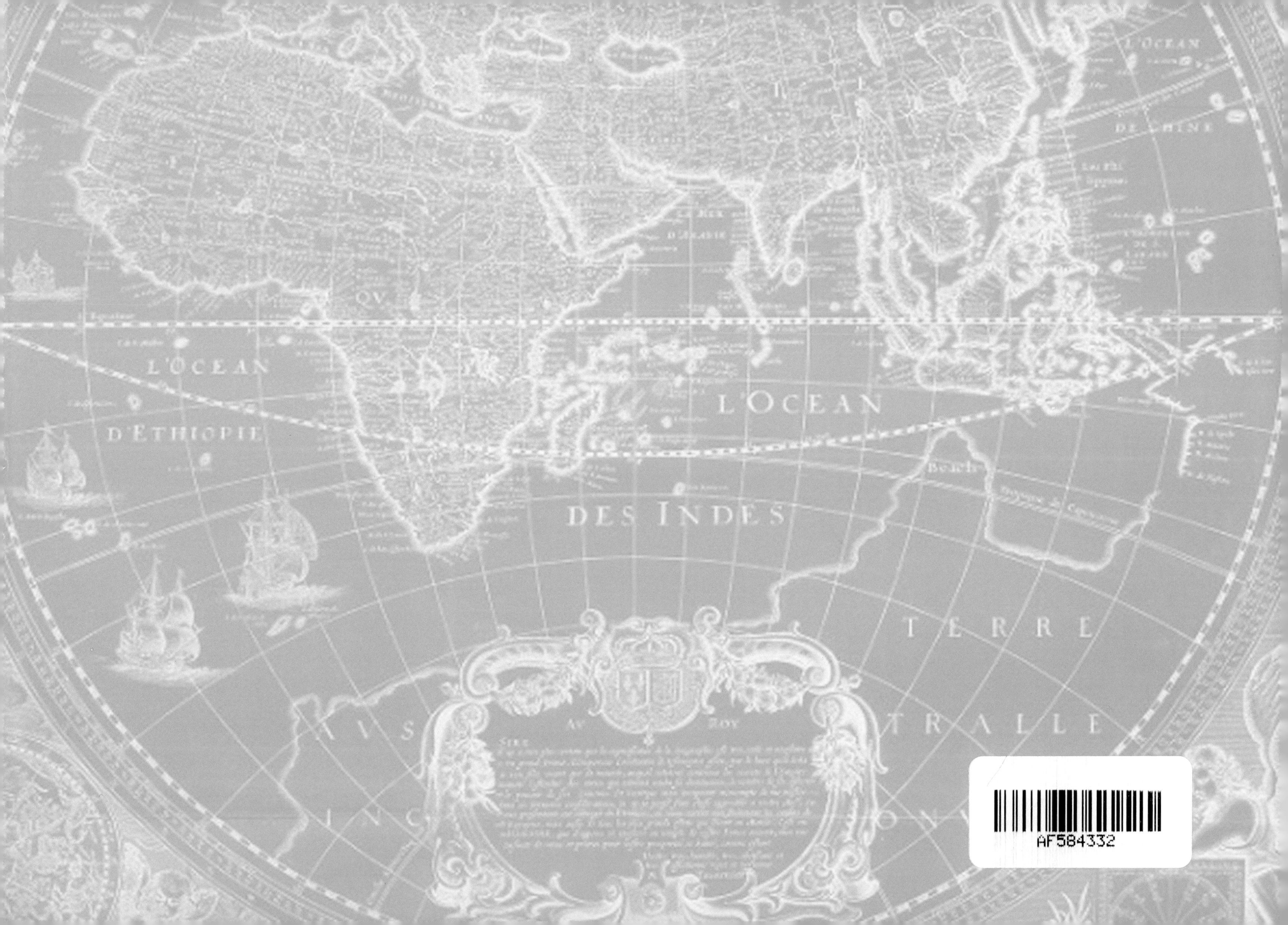

L'OCEAN
DE CHINE
L'OCEAN
D'ETHIOPIE
L'OCEAN
DES INDES
TERRE
AVS
TRALLE
AV ROY
SIRE

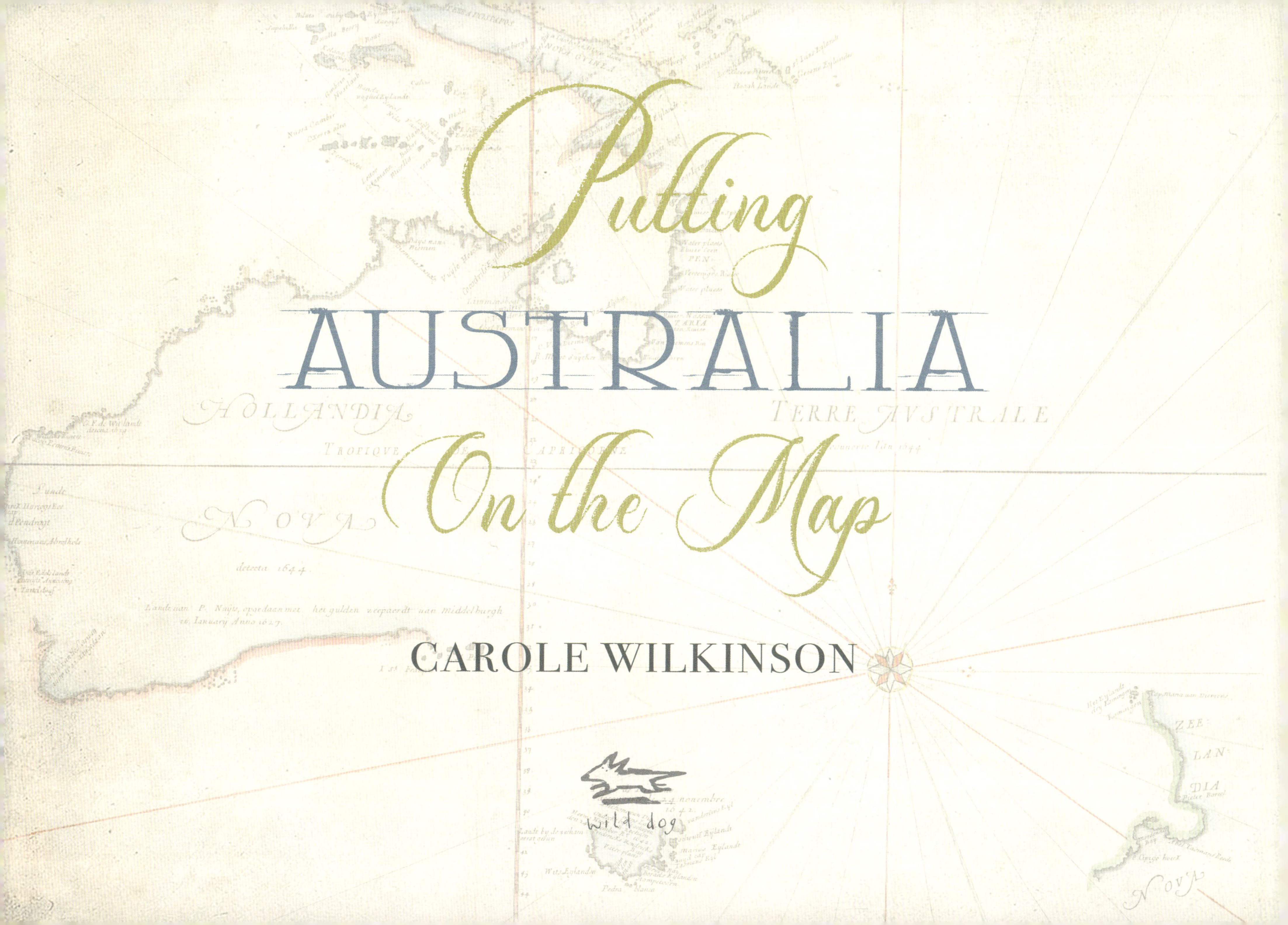

Putting AUSTRALIA On the Map

CAROLE WILKINSON

wild dog

First published in 2020 by

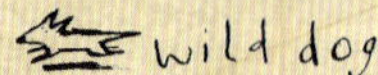

Abbotsford Convent
1 St Heliers Street
Abbotsford Vic 3067
Australia
+61 3 9419 9406
admin@wdog.com.au
wdog.com.au

Printed and bound in China by Everbest Printing Co. Ltd

ISBN: 9781742035932

A catalogue record for this book is available from the National Library of Australia

Wild Dog would like to thank Neil Conning for his careful fact checking and thorough proofreading.

10 9 8 7 6 5 4 3 2 1   20 21 22 23 24

FSC® is a non-profit international organisation established to promote the responsible management of the world's forests.

PICTURE CREDITS

Images courtesy of National Library of Australia
Front cover Melchisédech Thévenot, NLA, MAP NK 2785; p 1 Melchisédech Thévenot, NLA, MAP NK 2785; p 14 Vincenzo Coronelli, NLA, MAP NK 10240; p 17 Hessel Gerritsz, NLA, MAP RM 750; 18 Melchisédech Thévenot, NLA, MAP NK 2785; p 23 William Dampier, NLA, NK1509; p 24 Richard Cushee, NLA, MAP GLOBE 6; p 27 James Cook, NLA, MAP T 325; p 31 Matthew Flinders, NLA, MAP T 1494; Back cover Melchisédech Thévenot, NLA, MAP NK 2785.

Images courtesy of State Library of Queensland
p 13 Public domain / Hessel Gerritsz.

Images courtesy of State Library of Victoria
p 28 Public domain / Samuel Calvert.

Images courtesy of Wikimedia Commons
pp 2-3 Public domain / Abel Janszoon Tasman; p 4 Public domain / Claudius Ptolemy; p 7 Public domain / Claudius Ptolemy; p 8 Public domain / Domingos Teixeira; p 11 Public domain / Petrus Plancius; p 21 Public domain / Thomas Murray; Endpapers Public domain / Melchior Tavernier.

Carole Wilkinson is an internationally award-winning and best-selling author. Her *Dragonkeeper* series has sold all over the world and is currently being made into a film. Carole's most recent non-fiction title, *10 Pound Pom*, won the 2018 Primary Educational Picture Book of the Year and was shortlisted for the 2018 CBCA Picture Book of the Year. Carole lives in Melbourne.

Contents

Introduction

ANCESTORS of Australia's First Nations People made the dangerous journey to Australia at least 50,000 years ago.

Australia is a big place. It covers 7.7 million square kilometres and its coastline is about 35,000 km long. You might think it would be easy to find, but it stayed hidden from the rest of the world for a very long time.

Australia's coastline was mapped piece by piece, put together like a jigsaw puzzle. Putting Australia on the map was a task that took navigators 200 years to achieve.

Insculptum est per Johannē Schnitzer de Armßheim
CAVRVS·CHORVS·VEL·IAPIX·SIVE·ARGESTES
CIRCIVS VEL TRESIIAS
SEPTENTRIO·VEL·APARCTIAS
AQVILO·VEL·BOREAS
CECIAS·APELIOTES
FAVONIVS·ZEPHIRVS
SVBSOLANVS
EVROPA
ASIA
LIBIA INTERIOR
AFRICA
ARABIA FELIX
ETHIOPIA INTERIOR
MARE·INDICVM
MARE·INDICVM
MARE
PRASODVM
Terra incognita secundū ptholomeum
Tropicus Capricorni
Gradus longitudinis ab occidente ad orientem
AFRICVS·VEL·LIBS
LIBONOTVS·EVROAVSTER
AVSTER·VEL·NOTVS
EVRNOTVS
VVLTVRNVS·EVRVS

Two Books

AROUND AD 150, Roman mathematician and astronomer Claudius Ptolemy wrote a book called *Geography*. It included his calculations of latitude and longitude for 8000 places. These places, mainly in Europe, occupied just a quarter of the globe. Ptolemy had no knowledge of the rest of the world. He believed the Southern Hemisphere was mostly land, to balance all the land in the Northern Hemisphere.

Marco Polo was an Italian adventurer and merchant who travelled to China from 1271 to 1295. He wrote a book about his travels called *Book of the Marvels of the World*. He described previously unknown places, including Maletur, where great quantities of spices grew, and Iocathe, which had vast amounts of gold as well as many elephants.

For hundreds of years, these books inspired people to explore the world. But neither Ptolemy nor Marco Polo provided maps to show how to find these exotic places.

OPPOSITE: Map of the known world in 1482, drawn using Ptolemy's coordinates.

Empty Southern Hemisphere

PTOLEMY'S *Geography* was rediscovered by European scholars in the 14th century, and cartographers used his coordinates to draw maps. Three-quarters of the world, including the entire Southern Hemisphere, was still unknown.

Cartographers didn't like empty spaces on their maps. Some populated the empty oceans with sea monsters. Others filled the bottom of their maps with a large land mass, just as Ptolemy had suggested. They called it *Terra Australis Incognita* or Unknown South Land.

Over many years, Polo's book was copied and recopied by hand. Mistakes crept in. Iocathe became Lochac, and then Beach. No one had found these places, so cartographers put them on the Unknown South Land.

OPPOSITE: 1540 map of the world from *Cosmography*, a book by a German cartographer, showing sea monsters in the southern oceans.

TYPVS ORBIS VNIVERSALIS

POLVS.ARTICVS
TERA NOVA
TEMPERADA.ZONA
MARNEGRO
CIRCVLVS.CANCRI
MARPANAMA
TORIDA.ZONA
TORIDA.ZONA
CIRCVLVS.CAPRICORNIO
MARDOSVL
TEMPERADA.ZONA
OCIDENTE
ANTILHAS
MAR OCCEANO
PERV
BRASIL
EQVINOCIAL
MVNDVS NOVVS
ESTREITO DE FERNÃ DE MAGALHAES
MOSCOVIA
EVROPA
TVRQVIA
MAR CASPIO
IERVSALEM
IAPAN
ACHINA
PARTES DAFRICA
CASTEL DAMINA
CONGO
CEILAM
MARDAINDIA
SAN LOURENCO
CABO.BOA.ESPERAÇA
DOMINGOS TEIXEIRA
1573
ORIENTE
POLOS ANTARTICVS

Rivals Rule the Waves

SPAIN AND PORTUGAL were racing each other to find new lands with rich resources such as gold and spices. Today, we buy spices such as nutmeg, cinnamon and ginger at the supermarket. In past times, they were rare luxuries. Pepper was worth more than gold. Spices grew only on a few islands in the East Indies, which became known as the Spice Islands.

While Spanish and Portuguese explorers were searching for quicker routes to this treasure trove, they discovered North and South America. They extended the map of the world into the Southern Hemisphere. But despite many theories about Portuguese ships discovering Australia, there is no evidence they ever did.

In 1520, Portuguese explorer Ferdinand Magellan sailed south and found a way around the bottom of South America into the Pacific Ocean. He and most of his crew were killed in the Philippines. Juan Sebastian Elcano and other survivors continued the voyage. They came close to Australia when they sailed past Timor on their voyage home.

Pedro Fernandes de Quirós was a Portuguese navigator who worked for the Spanish government. In 1519, with a fleet of three ships, he sailed west from Peru across the Pacific Ocean. Unlike other explorers, Quirós was actually looking for the Unknown South Land. He wanted to set up a colony there and populate it with Catholics from Spain.

In 1606, Quirós came across a coastline in the Pacific Ocean and

OPPOSITE: 1573 Portuguese map of the world with North America taking shape but with no sign of Australia.

was certain he had found the edge of the Unknown South Land. He named it Australia del Espiritu Santo (Southern Land of the Holy Ghost). When his fleet was separated in a storm, Quirós abandoned his other ships and sailed to a safe port.

Spanish sailor Luis de Vaez Torres was commander of the second-largest ship. After Quirós disappeared, Torres sailed around Australia del Espiritu Santo, and discovered it was a small island (part of present-day Vanuatu).

Torres had secret instructions from the Spanish government to be opened only if something happened to Quirós. They ordered him to continue searching for the Unknown South Land.

Torres kept sailing westward. He was heading straight for Australia. Then, following his orders, he turned north and sailed to the Philippines. He had come within 500 km of Australia's eastern coast. He sailed through the channel between New Guinea and Cape York, which was later named Torres Strait after him. Torres glimpsed the tip of Cape York, but decided it was another island.

The Spanish were secretive about their discoveries. Torres's charts disappeared into their archives. It would be a long time before anyone else found the elusive Torres Strait.

Ptolemy had been wrong when he said the Southern Hemisphere must contain a lot of land. Actually it is more than 80 per cent ocean.

Australia lay sprawled between the Indian and the Pacific Oceans, but the world's greatest explorers failed to find it.

However, another nation was sailing the high seas.

OPPOSITE: 1594 Dutch map of the world, with a large *Terra Australis* in the Southern Hemisphere. Marco Polo's Beach and Maletur have been placed on a peninsula.

ORBIS TERRARVM TYPVS DE INTEGRO MULTIS IN LOCIS EMENDATUS auctore Petro Plancio 1594.
EUROPA
ASIA
MEXICANA
PERUANA
MAGALLANICA
AFRICA
Circulus Aequinoctialis
Tropicus Capricorni
Circulus Antarcticus
Polus Antarcticus
TERRA AUSTRALIS
MAGALLANICA
OCEANVS TARTARICUS

The First Piece of the Puzzle

THE COUNTRY we call the Netherlands began as a small group of provinces in western Europe ruled by Spain. By 1606, it was a new republic that wanted a share of the spice trade.

The Netherlands didn't have a rich king like the Spanish and Portuguese to pay for voyages of exploration, so Dutch merchants joined forces. They formed the Vereenigde Oost-Indische Compagnie (United East India Company), known as the VOC for short.

Captain Willem Janszoon set out in a VOC ship called the *Duyfken* to explore the coast of New Guinea for trade opportunities. He sailed along its southern coast, passing what he thought was a large bay littered with reefs and small islands. It wasn't. It was a strait — the same one Torres would sail through a few months later. Janszoon believed that the next stretch of land he saw was a continuation of the coast of New Guinea. But the *Duyfken* was actually sailing along the western coast of Cape York.

Janzoon and his crew went ashore, and became the first recorded Europeans to set foot on Australia. They just didn't know it.

Janzoon and his crew were also the first Europeans to encounter Australia's First Nations People, who fiercely defended their country. There were deaths on both sides.

Janszoon drew a chart of more than 300 km of Cape York coast. It was the first small piece of Australia to be put on any map.

OPPOSITE: Dutch map of the Pacific Ocean, 1622, with the first small piece of Australia on a map. It is labelled *Nueva Guinea* – New Guinea.

MAR NEGRO
MAR DEL SVR
MAR PACIFICO
LA FLORIDA
QVIBIRA
TARTARIA
SINA
ARCHIPELAGO DE S. LAZARO
Filipinas
Islas de Salomon
Linea Æquinoctialis dat is de Middellyn
Tropicus Cancri dat is Creefts Sonnewend of Noorder Sonnestandt
Tropicus Capricorni dat is Steenbocx Sonnewend of Zuyder Sonnestandt

Isolario del P. Coronelli.

Accidental Discovery

WHILE THE PORTUGUESE and the Spanish were competing for control of the Spice Islands, the Dutch moved in. The VOC set up its headquarters in Batavia (present day Jakarta) on the island of Java. Portugal's power faded. The Spanish concentrated on their conquests in the Americas.

Sailing close to the coasts of Africa and India, the voyage from the Netherlands to the Spice Islands took a year or more.

Then a Dutch navigator discovered that by sailing directly east from the southern tip of Africa he could pick up fierce westerly winds (known as the Roaring Forties). They would speed his ship across the Indian Ocean before he turned north to head to Batavia. This cut the journey time in half. The VOC ordered all their ships to take the quicker route.

The problem was that a reliable way of measuring longitude hadn't been invented. Navigators didn't know when they'd reached the longitude of Batavia. A number of ships overshot their mark and ended up on Australia's wild western coast.

Some ships were wrecked there, and others came in search of survivors. Over the next century at least 40 Dutch ships reached the coast of Australia.

OPPOSITE: Section of a 1628 Dutch globe showing northern New Holland, depicting the cartographer's ideas of the inhabitants as well as its animals, which included deer and an elephant.

A Corner of a Continent

IN 1606, Dirk Hartog was the first Dutch navigator to unintentionally reach the west coast of Australia, on board the *Eendracht*. He anchored in Shark Bay 700 km north of Perth and rowed to a small island carrying a pewter dinner plate from the ship's galley. The plate, engraved with an account of their landing, was nailed to a post. Hartog gave Australia its first name — Eendrachtsland. The name never caught on.

More Dutch sailors reached the treacherous shores of Australia, charting stretches of the western and southern coasts.

In 1628, the VOC's chief cartographer, Hessel Gerritsz, pieced together bits of the coast charted by eight Dutch navigators. He'd created the first map of Australia, not to help sailors find it, but so they could avoid its treacherous coasts.

The VOC tried to keep the chart hidden from rival companies, but it wasn't long before this coast appeared on maps of the world.

The newly discovered land was now vying for space with the imagined land around the bottom of the world. There was confusion about what to call them. The sensible Dutch came up with a solution. They called the place their navigators had actually discovered the Known South Land. The mythical world of gold and spices, which they still hoped to find, they called the Unknown South Land.

OPPOSITE: Chart of Dutch sailors' discoveries of western and southern Australia between 1616 and 1628, drawn by VOC chief cartographer Hessel Gerritsz.

Tropicus Capricorni
G.F. de Wits landt
't Land van d'Eendraght
I. d'Edels landt
't Land van de Leeuwin
't Landt van P. Nuyts
Menij

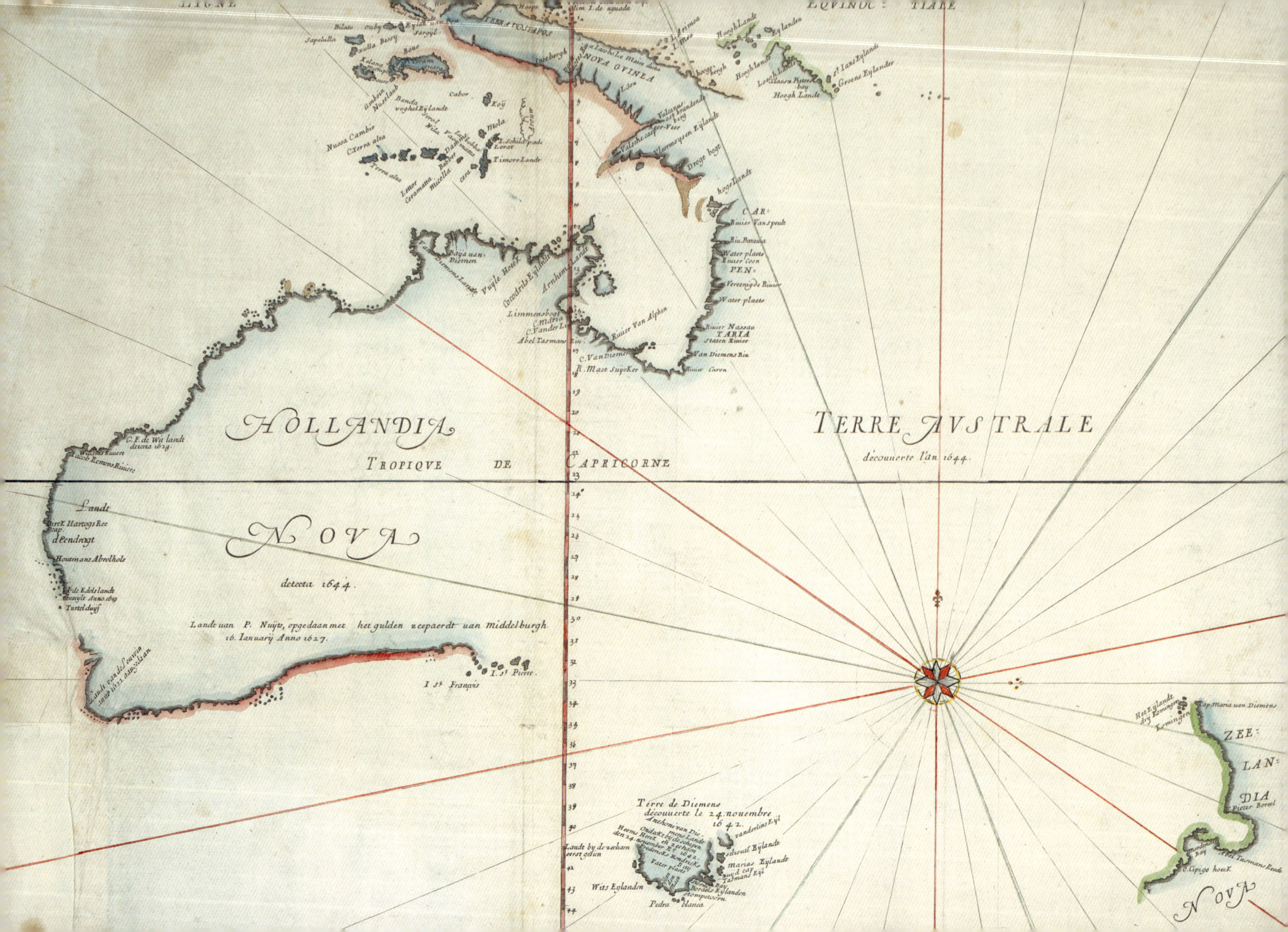

NOVA GVINEA
CAR
PEN
TARIA
HOLLANDIA
TROPIQVE DE CAPRICORNE
NOVA
detecta 1644
TERRE AVSTRALE
decouuerte l'an 1644
Landt uan P. Nuijts, opgedaan met het gulden zeepaerdt uan Middelburgh
16. January Anno 1627.
I. St. Pierre
I. St. Francois
Houtmans Abrolhols
Turtelduyf
Terre de Diemens
decouuerte le 24 nouembre
1642.
ZEE-
LAN-
DIA
NOVA

Island or Mainland?

IN 1642, the governor of the VOC, Anthony van Diemen, commissioned a major Dutch exploration to learn about the mysterious Known South Land. Was it attached to the Unknown South Land or New Guinea? Was there a sea route around it that led to the Pacific Ocean? And of course he wanted to know if there were natural resources that could be sold to the world. The VOC had a list of things they were looking for — gold, silver, tin, iron, lead and copper; precious stones, pearls, vegetables and fruits. Sailors were told to observe the Indigenous people for clues. Were they wearing ornaments of gold and silver?

Abel Janszoon Tasman was commander of the voyage. Sailing further south than other mariners, he didn't see the west or the south coast of Australia. The first land he came to he named Anthony van Diemen's Land, after his sponsor. He didn't know whether it was an island or joined to the mainland. It would be 200 years before this place he had discovered would be named after him — Tasmania.

Tasman was a great seaman, but a rather timid explorer. He and his crew were all fearful of the inhabitants of Van Diemen's Land. Perhaps because the VOC's instructions told them to look out for the "fierce savages" that were known to live in southern regions.

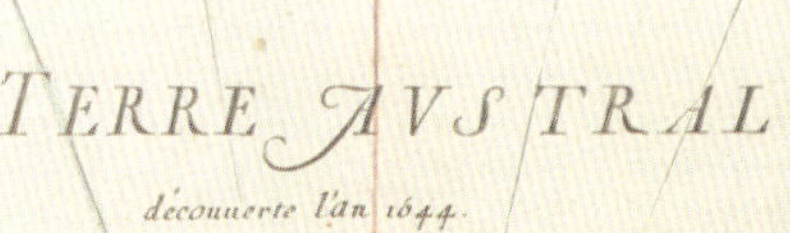

OPPOSITE: 1663 French map including Tasman's discoveries, which suggests New Guinea, Van Diemen's Land and New Zealand could all be part of New Holland.

TERRE AVSTRALE

Tasman didn't set foot on Van Diemen's Land himself. Instead he sent some nervous crewmen. They found notches in a tree, which they thought were made for climbing. As they were 150 cm apart, they decided that the inhabitants must be very tall.

Tasman sailed around the southern coast of Van Diemen's Land, but the seas were too rough to anchor close to shore. Instead, he ordered the ship's carpenter to swim ashore with a pole and a Dutch flag to mark their discovery. Tasman gave the continent its second name — New Holland, which was used for almost 200 years.

Tasman sailed on and became the first European to discover New Zealand. His voyage was of great interest to sailors and cartographers, but Van Diemen was unimpressed. Tasman had proved that New Holland wasn't a part of a massive Unknown South Land, but he hadn't found anything of value to trade. Despite these disappointing results, in 1644 Tasman was commissioned to command a second voyage to New Holland. VOC officials were still hoping that Marco Polo's Beach with its abundant gold might be discovered there. This time, Tasman sailed along the northern coast. It was another unprofitable voyage.

The VOC lost interest in New Holland.

An English Pirate

BRITISH EXPLORATION of Australia got off to a bad start. In 1622, the ship *Tryall* was wrecked off the Western Australian coast, with the loss of more than 90 men and a cargo of silver.

The first Englishman to set foot on Australia was William Dampier. His earliest experience at sea was on pirate ships. In 1688, he became a privateer and spent three months on the

LEFT: William Dampier holding his best-selling book.

A MAP OF THE WORLD. Shewing the Course of M^r. DAMPIERS Voyage Round it: From 1679. to 1691

north-western coast of Australia. He was the first explorer to take a scientific interest in Australia, drawing the plants, animals and Aboriginal people he encountered.

Dampier was perplexed by Australia's Aboriginal people. He couldn't understand why they didn't envy the British way of life, or why they didn't admire their possessions. He didn't know that Australia's First Nations People had tens of thousands of years of experience managing their land, which provided everything they needed.

When he returned to England, Dampier wrote a book about his adventures. It became a best seller. The British Navy was impressed. Ignoring his shady past, they commissioned Dampier to command the *Roebuck*. In 1699, he set out to explore the eastern coast of New Holland. Unfortunately, the *Roebuck* was in terrible condition.

Dampier sailed along the northern coast of Australia. Like other explorers, he couldn't find enough water. Near Broome, he gave up and headed home. By this time, the *Roebuck* was so unseaworthy that Dampier and his crew were sure she was about to sink. They ran her aground on Ascension Island before she sank. They were marooned there for five weeks. Dampier never reached the east coast of Australia.

OPPOSITE: Map from Dampier's book, showing his voyages from 1679 to 1694.

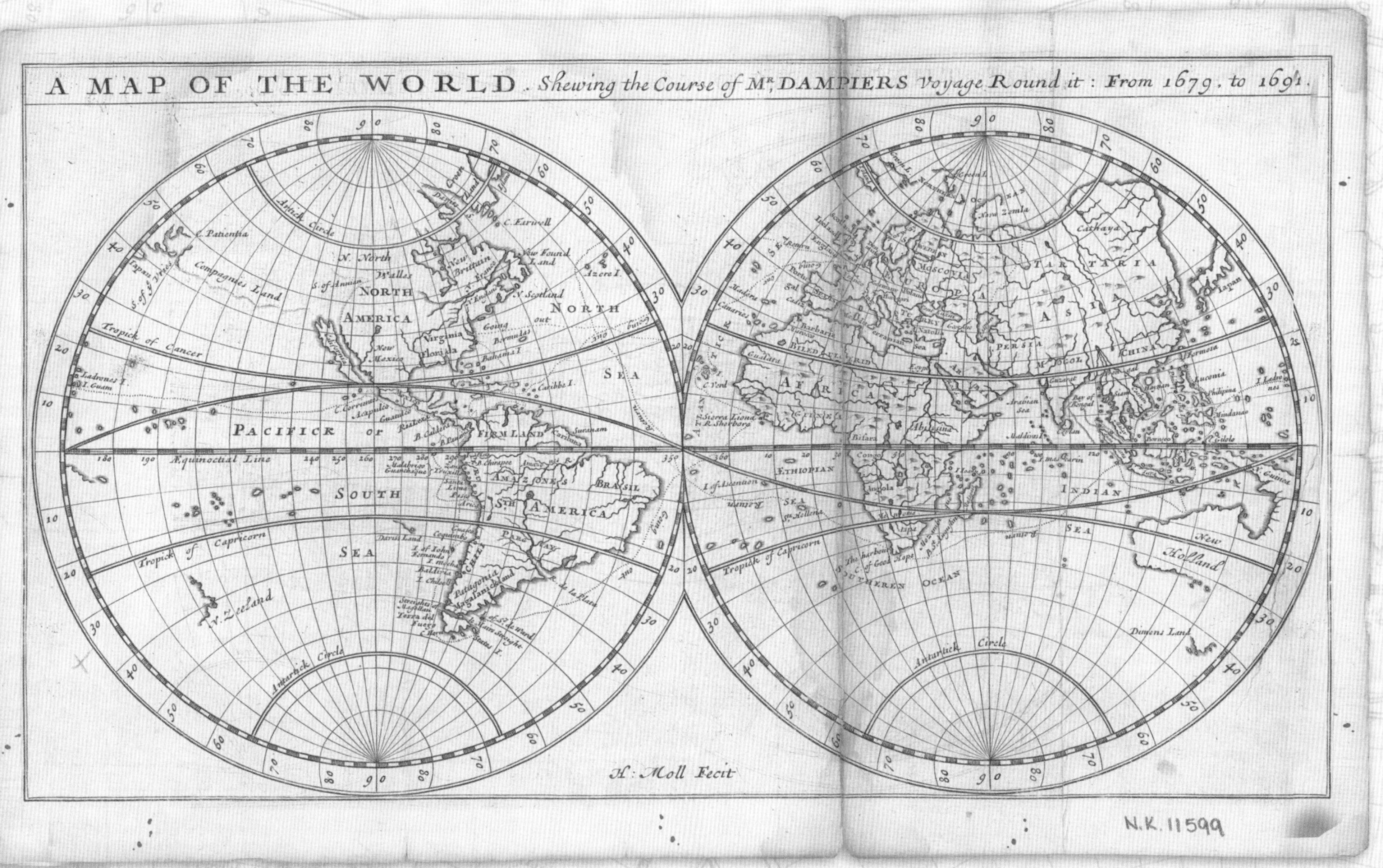
A MAP OF THE WORLD. Shewing the Course of Mr. DAMPIERS Voyage Round it: From 1679. to 1691.
NORTH AMERICA
PACIFICK or
SOUTH SEA
NORTH SEA
Tropick of Cancer
Tropick of Capricorn
Æquinoctial Line
Artick Circle
Antarctick Circle
AMAZONE'S
BRASIL
Sth AMERICA
N. Zeeland
ASIA
TARTARIA
EUROPA
AFRICA
PERSIA
CHINA
ETHIOPIAN SEA
INDIAN SEA
SOUTHERN OCEAN
New Holland
Dimens Land
H: Moll Fecit

IMAGINING THE EAST COAST

AS NEW HOLLAND took shape on the map, some cartographers joined it to the imaginary Unknown South Land. But that mythical land gradually shrank in size, eventually disappearing from world maps. One of the few remaining mysteries was the eastern coast of Australia.

In 1681, a magnificent globe of the world, 3.84 metres in diameter and weighing 1500 kilograms was made for French king Louis XIV. Its creator, Italian cartographer Vincenzo Coronelli showed the eastern coast of Australia blurring into the Pacific Ocean.

Others cartographers preferred to imagine what it looked like. With no evidence at all, they attached Van Diemen's Land to the mainland. Some decided to place Quirós's Espiritu Santo on the unexplored east coast. In the mid-1700s, English cartographer Richard Cushee drew a large bulge into the Pacific Ocean in an attempt to fit it on the map of Australia. Around the same time, the Dutch included a smaller bulge on a stone map of the world inlaid in the floor of their magnificent town hall in Amsterdam. It is still there today.

RIGHT: Richard Cushee globe showing bulge on the east coast.

Cook Arrives

IN 1768, the British Navy commissioned Lieutenant James Cook to sail the barque *Endeavour* to the South Seas to observe a rare astronomical event — the transit of Venus across the face of the Sun. He also had sealed secret orders. The navy wanted Cook to search for a "Continent or Land of great extent" in the Pacific Ocean.

Despite 150 years of evidence to the contrary, the British still hoped the Unknown South Land existed.

Cook sailed across the Pacific Ocean to New Zealand, and discovered that it was two islands. He saw no sign of the Unknown South Land.

Charting the unexplored east coast of New Holland was not in his instructions, but he sailed home via the East Indies. That took him along the east coast, where he got his first glimpse of Australia.

Ten days later, on 29 April 1770, Cook and his ship's company stepped onto Australian soil. Cook was more impressed by the continent than other explorers had been. Botanist Joseph Banks was so delighted by the new species of plants he found that Cook named the place Botany Bay. There were encounters with Aboriginal people, who clearly didn't want these strangers to land. They retreated when Cook fired his musket.

As the *Endeavour* sailed up the east coast, Cook charted it for the first time. He called it New South Wales.

Torres's account of discovering the strait between New Guinea and Australia had been so well hidden, that even the Spanish had forgotten about it. But it had been recently unearthed. Cook may have read it. When the *Endeavour* reached the tip of Cape York, he rediscovered the Torres Strait.

With a party of men, he went ashore on a small island and climbed a hill. From that vantage point Cook was reassured that there was a safe passage through. While they were there, he claimed New South Wales for the King of England. To mark the occasion a flag was raised and a volley of shots was fired. Ignoring the fact that New South Wales was obviously inhabited, the British declared it *Terra Nullius* – nobody's land. They now considered it theirs.

Cook charted the Torres Strait. On the map of the world, New Guinea was set free from the mainland. Van Diemen's Land, however, remained firmly attached.

OPPOSITE: Lieutenant James Cook's chart of the east coast of Australia. It is drawn with north to the right.

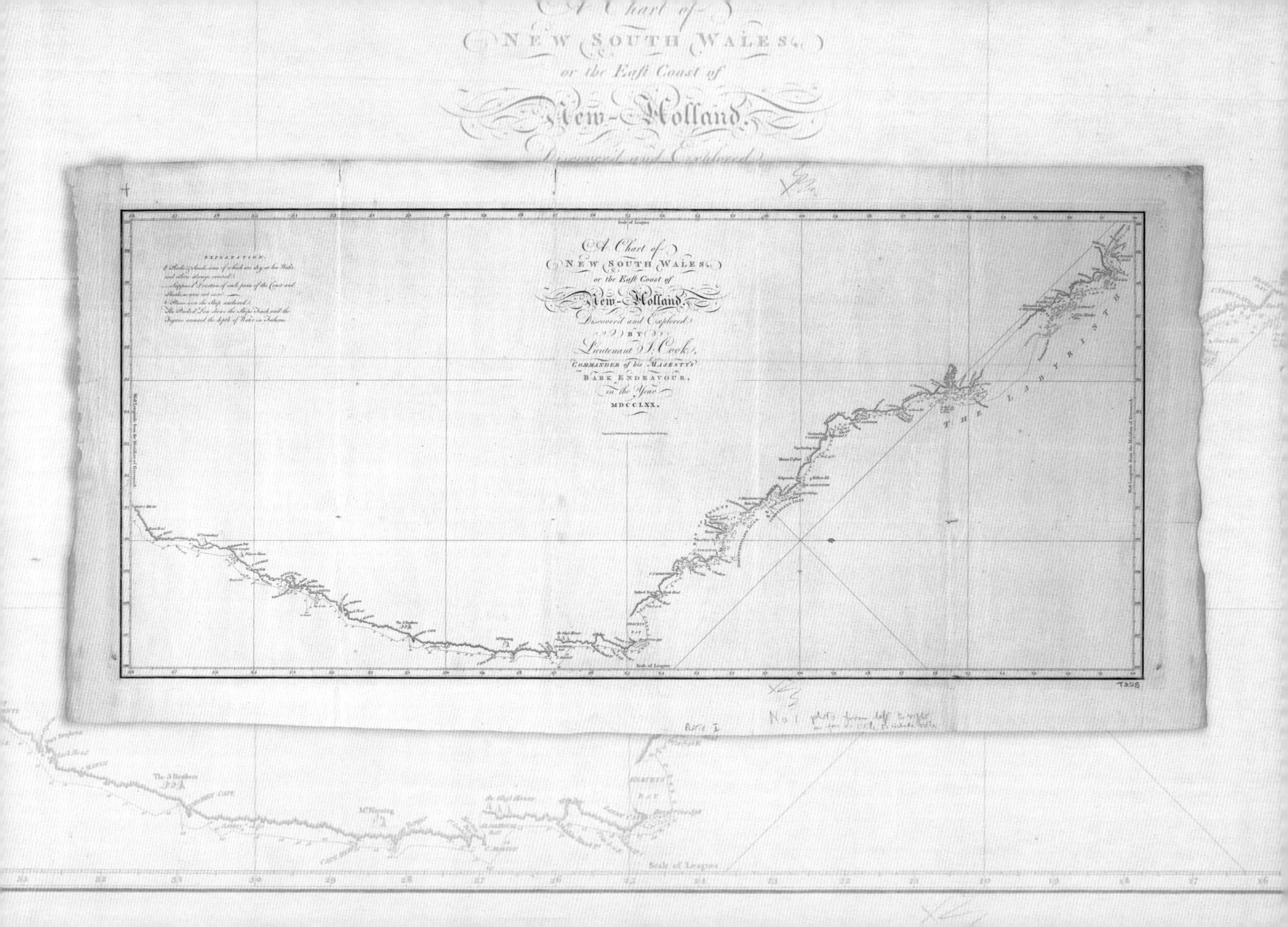

A Chart of
NEW SOUTH WALES,
or the East Coast of
New-Holland.
Discover'd and Explored

Scale of Leagues

A Chart of NEW SOUTH WALES, or the East Coast of New-Holland.

Discover'd and Explored

BY

Lieutenant J. Cook,

COMMANDER of his MAJESTY'S BARK ENDEAVOUR,

in the Year

MDCCLXX.

EXPLANATION.

Rocks & Sands, some of which are dry at low Water and others always covered.

Supposed Direction of such parts of the Coast and Shoals as were not seen.

Places were the Ship anchored.

The Pricked Line shews the Ships Track and the Figures annexed the depth of Water in Fathoms.

THE LABYRINTH

Scale of Leagues

T325

PLATE I

No 1 photo from left to right

The 3 Brothers

Mt Warning

Scale of Leagues

BRITISH COLONISATION

MANY NAVIGATORS had helped to chart Australia's coastline. The puzzle pieces were all in place. The map was more or less complete. But with its lack of water and trade goods, no nation had thought it was worth colonising.

British prisons were overflowing. Sir Joseph Banks suggested that New South Wales would be the perfect place for a convict settlement. There was concern that the Netherlands had claim to it, but despite marking their landings with plaques and flags, the Dutch had never made a formal claim on any part of Australia.

On 26 January 1788, Australia's first European citizens arrived — more than 700 unwanted convicts.

OPPOSITE: Cook's Possession Ceremony, as imagined in the *Sydney Illustrated News*, 1865.

FLINDERS FINISHES THE MAP

ABOVE: Portrait of Captain Matthew Flinders, by Toussaint Antoine de Chazal.

OPPOSITE: Matthew Flinders' *General Chart of Terra Australis, or Australia*, first published in 1814.

ACCURATE CHARTING of the coast of Australia was put on hold until a young Englishman named Matthew Flinders came along. He wanted to sail the oceans and add to the knowledge of the world.

Flinders' first voyage to the colony of New South Wales was as a midshipman on the *Reliance* in 1795. When on leave from his duties, he and his friend George Bass borrowed a small ship and sailed all the way around Van Diemen's Land. Almost 150 years after Tasman first discovered it, these two young men finally proved it was an island.

In 1801, Flinders returned to New South Wales in command of the *Investigator*, on a voyage to explore the coastline in detail. He charted the final section of the southern coast and circumnavigated the continent, correcting errors on previous charts.

Australia was finally on the world map — all of it.

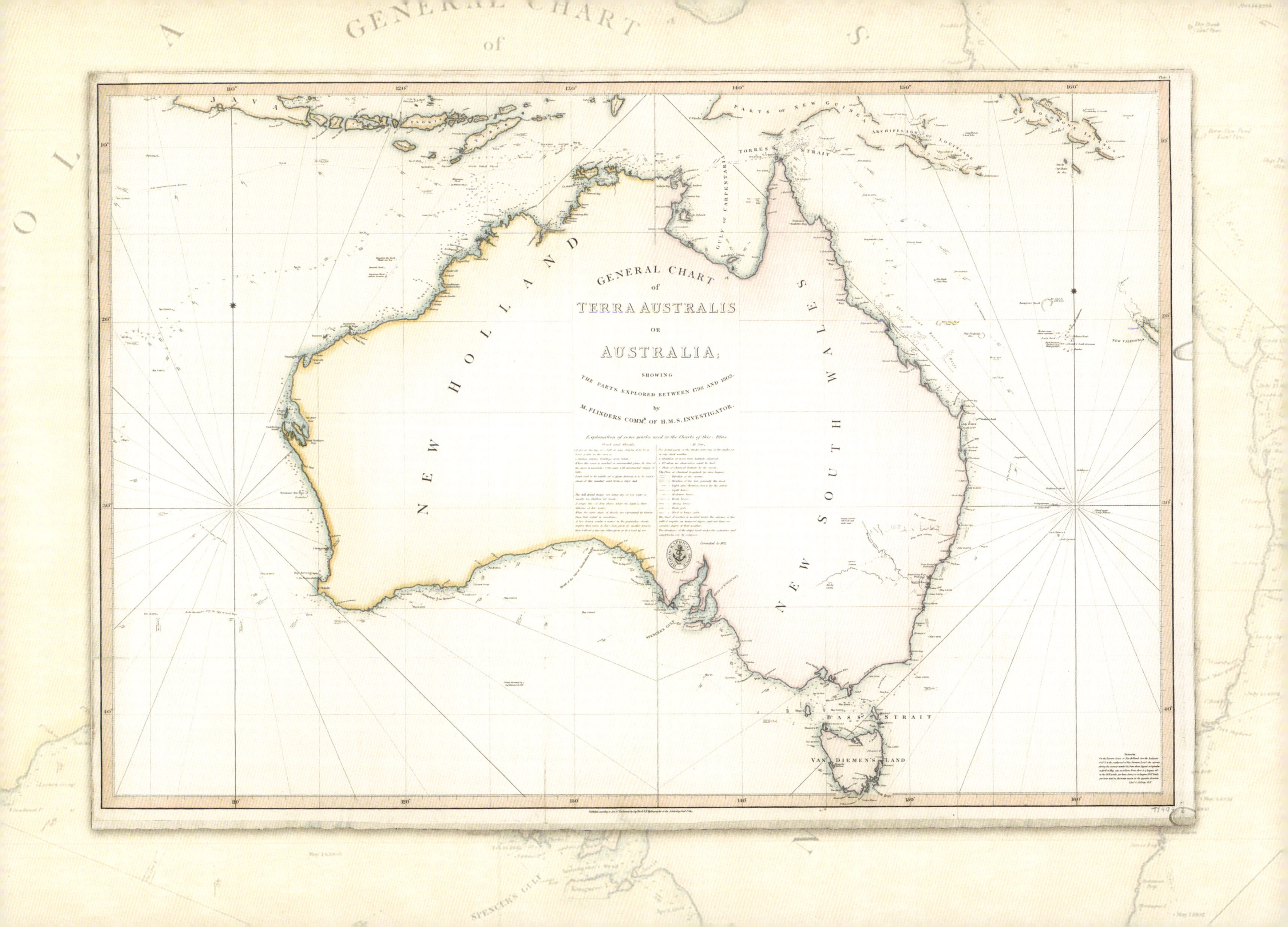

GENERAL CHART
of
TERRA AUSTRALIS
OR
AUSTRALIA;
SHOWING
THE PARTS EXPLORED BETWEEN 1798 AND 1803.
by
M. FLINDERS COMMR. OF H.M.S. INVESTIGATOR.

Explanation of some marks used in the Charts of this Atlas.

HYDROGRAPHICAL OFFICE

JAVA

FLORES

TIMOR

PARTS OF NEW GUINEA

ARCHIPELAGO OF LOUISIADE

SOLOMON ISLANDS

TORRES STRAIT

GULF OF CARPENTARIA

NEW HOLLAND

NEW SOUTH WALES

NEW CALEDONIA

SPENCER'S GULF

GULF OF ST VINCENT

BASS STRAIT

VAN DIEMEN'S LAND

110° 120° 130° 140° 150° 160°

10° 20° 30° 40°

Glossary

ANCESTORS: People from whom one's parents are descended.

ARCHIVE: A place in which public records or historical papers are stored.

ASTRONOMER: Someone who studies the stars and planets.

CARTOGRAPHER: Someone who creates or draws maps.

CIRCUMNAVIGATE: To travel completely around something, usually by ship or plane.

COLONY: A group of people who settle in a place far from home but are governed by their homeland.

COMMISSIONED: Given the rank of officer in the navy.

COORDINATES: A group of numbers used to indicate a location on a map.

ELUSIVE: Something which is difficult to define or capture.

LATITUDE AND LONGITUDE: A system of lines used to describe the position of any place on Earth. Lines of latitude are positions north or south of the equator. Lines of longitude are positions east or west, usually measured as the distance from Greenwich in England.

MARINER: Sailor, a person who navigates or assists in navigating a ship.

MAROONED: To be put ashore in a place from which it is difficult to escape.

MERCHANT: A person who buys and sells goods.

MIDSHIPMAN: A person who is training to become an officer in the navy.

MUSKET: A heavy long-barrelled gun, pre-dating the rifle.

PERPLEXED: Unable to understand something clearly.

PEWTER: A metal made mostly of tin that is used in making utensils.

PRIVATEER: An officer or crew member on a privately owned and armed ship permitted by a government to make war on enemy ships.

PROVINCE: A part of a country that has its own government.

TERRA NULLIUS: A Latin expression which means "land belonging to no one".

VOLLEY: Shots fired by a number of firearms at the same time.

Index

AME
LA MER
DV
NORT
LA MER
DV
SVD
RI
QVE